I0880638

REPENTANCE

REPENTANCE

What it Means to Repent
and Why We Must Do So

J. C. RYLE

ANEKO
PRESS

We love hearing from our readers. Please contact us at www.anekopress.com/questions-comments with any questions, comments, or suggestions.

Repentance

© 2021 by Aneko Press

All rights reserved. First edition 1878.

Updated edition 2021

No part of this book may be reproduced, stored in a retrieval system, or transmitted in any form or by any means – electronic, mechanical, photocopying, recording, or otherwise, without written permission from the publisher.

Scripture quotations from The Authorized (King James) Version. Rights in the Authorized Version in the United Kingdom are vested in the Crown. Reproduced by permission of the Crown's patentee, Cambridge University Press.

Cover Design: Jonathan Lewis

Editor: Paul Miller

Aneko Press

www.anekopress.com

Aneko Press, Life Sentence Publishing, and our logos are trademarks of

Life Sentence Publishing, Inc.

203 E. Birch Street

P.O. Box 652

Abbotsford, WI 54405

RELIGION / Christian Theology / General

Paperback ISBN: 978-1-62245-746-5

eBook ISBN: 978-1-62245-747-2

10 9 8 7 6 5 4 3 2

Available where books are sold

Contents

Introduction ix

Section 1: What is Repentance? 1

Section 2: Why is Repentance Necessary? 9

Section 3: What is There to Lead a Person to Repent? 21

Conclusion 31

J. C. Ryle – A Brief Biography 43

Other Similar Titles 49

Introduction

*Except you repent, you will all
likewise perish.* Luke 13:3

The text seems stern and severe at first: *Except you repent, you will all likewise perish.* I can imagine someone asking, "Is this the gospel? Are these the glad tidings? Are these the good news of which ministers speak?" *This is a hard saying; who can hear it?* (John 6:60).

From whose lips did these words come, though? They came from the lips of One who loves us with a love that passes knowledge. They came from Jesus Christ, the Son of God. They were spoken by One who loved us so much that He left heaven for our sakes. He came down to earth for our sakes. He lived a poor, humble life on earth for thirty-three years for our sakes. He went to the cross for us, went to the grave for us, and died for our sins. The words that come from lips like these must surely be words of love.

After all, what greater proof of love can be given than to warn a friend of coming danger? The father most certainly loves his son who sees him heading toward the edge of a cliff and cries out, "Stop, stop!" The tender mother certainly loves her child who sees her young one about to eat a poisonous berry and yells, "Stop! Stop! Put it down!"

It is indifference that leaves people alone and allows them to go their own way. It is love, tender love, that warns them and raises the cry of alarm. The cry of "Fire! Fire!" at midnight might sometimes rudely, harshly, and unpleasantly startle a person out of his sleep, but who would complain if that cry was the means of saving his life? The words *Except you repent, you will all likewise perish* might at first seem stern and severe, but they are words of love, and they could be the means of delivering precious souls from hell.

There are three things I want you to pay attention to from this text of Scripture:

1. The **nature** of repentance: What is it?

2. The **necessity** of repentance: Why is repentance needful?

3. The **encouragements** to repentance: What is there to lead people to repent?

Section 1

What is Repentance?

L et us be sure to set down our feet firmly on this point. The importance of the question cannot be overrated. Repentance is one of the foundation stones of Christianity. We find repentance spoken of in the New Testament at least sixty times.

What was the first doctrine our Lord Jesus Christ preached? We are told that He said, *Repent, and believe the gospel* (Mark 1:15). What did the apostles proclaim when the Lord sent them forth the first time? They *preached that people should repent* (Mark 6:12). What was the instruction that Jesus gave His disciples when He left the world? He said that *repentance and remission of sins should be preached in His name among all nations* (Luke 24:47).

What was the concluding appeal of the first sermons that Peter preached? *Repent, and be baptized.... Repent you, and be converted* (Acts 2:38; 3:19). What was the summary of doctrine that Paul gave to the Ephesian elders right before he left them? He told them that he had taught them publicly, and from house to house, *testifying both to the Jews, and also to the Greeks, repentance toward God, and faith toward our Lord Jesus Christ* (Acts 20:21). What was the description that Paul gave of his own ministry when he made his defense before Festus and Agrippa? He told them that he had taught all people that they should *repent, and do works fit for repentance* (Acts 26:20). What was the account given by the believers at Jerusalem regarding the conversion of the gentiles? When they heard of it, they said, *Then has God also to the gentiles granted repentance unto life* (Acts 11:18).

What is one of the first qualifications that the Church of England requires of all people who desire to come to the Lord's table? They are to "examine themselves whether they repent them truly of their former sins." According to the Church of England, no unrepentant person should ever come to the Lord's table. Certainly we can all agree that these are all serious considerations. They should show the importance of the question I am now asking. A mistake about repentance is a most dangerous mistake. An error about repentance is an error that lies at the very root of our religion. What, then, is repentance? When can it be said of anyone that he repents?

Repentance is a thorough change of a person's natural heart regarding the subject of sin. We are all born in sin. We naturally love sin. We take to sin as

2

soon as we can act and think – just as the bird takes to flying and the fish takes to swimming. There never was a child who required schooling or education in order to learn deceitfulness, selfishness, anger, self-will, gluttony, pride, and foolishness. These things are not picked up from bad companions or gradually learned by a long course of tedious instruction. They show up on their own. The seeds of sin are evidently the natural product of the heart. The aptitude of all children to these evil things is an unanswerable proof of the corruption and fall of man.

However, when this heart of ours is changed by the Holy Spirit, when this natural love of sin is cast out, then that change takes place that the Word of God calls "repentance." The person in whom the change is made is said to "repent." He can be called a "penitent" or "repentant" person.

I do not want to end the subject here, though. It deserves a closer and more searching investigation. It is not safe to deal in general statements when doctrines of this kind are handled. I will try to take *repentance* apart and dissect and analyze it before your eyes. I will show you the parts and pieces of which repentance is made up. I will try to set before you something of the experience of every truly repentant person.

True repentance begins with knowledge of sin. The eyes of the repentant person are opened. He sees the length and breadth of God's holy law with distress and confusion. He sees the extent, the enormous extent, of his own transgressions. To his surprise, he discovers that he has been under a huge delusion by thinking of himself as a good person with a good heart. He learns that in reality he is wicked, guilty, corrupt, and evil in God's sight. His pride breaks down. His high thoughts melt away. He sees that he is a great sinner. This is the first step in true repentance.

True repentance produces sorrow for sin. The heart of a repentant person is touched with deep remorse because of his past sin and transgressions. He is cut to the heart to think that he has lived so foolishly and so wickedly. He mourns over wasted time, over abilities misused, over dishonoring God, and over injuring his own soul. The remembrance of these things is painful to him. The burden of these things is sometimes almost unbearable. When a person sorrows in this way, you have the second step in true repentance.

True repentance produces confession of sin. The tongue of a repentant person is loosed. He must speak to that God against whom he has sinned. Something within him tells him that he must cry to God, pray to God, and talk with God about the condition of his own soul. He must pour out his heart and acknowledge his iniquities at the throne of grace. They are a heavy burden within him, and he can no longer keep silent. He can keep nothing back. He will not hide anything. He goes before God, making no excuses and without trying to justify himself. He is willing to say, "I have sinned against heaven and before You; my iniquity is great. God, be merciful to me, a sinner!" When a person sincerely confesses to God in this way, you have the third step in true repentance.

True repentance leads to a thorough breaking off

from sin. The life of a repentant person is changed. The course of his daily conduct is entirely different. A new King reigns within his heart. He puts off the old nature. He now desires to do what God commands. He now desires to avoid what God forbids. He now strives to avoid sin in every way. He desires to fight with sin, to war with sin, and to get the victory over sin. He ceases to do evil. He learns to do good (Isaiah 1:16-17). He abruptly leaves bad ways and bad companions. He labors, however feebly, to live a new life. When a person does this, you have the fourth step in true repentance.

> The life of a repentant person is changed.

True repentance shows itself by producing in the heart an established habit of deep hatred of all sin. The mind of a repentant person becomes a mind that is habitually holy. He abhors that which is evil and clings to that which is good (Romans 12:9). He delights in the law of God (Romans 7:22). He often comes up short of his own desire to please and follow God. He finds in himself an evil principle warring against the spirit of God (Galatians 5:17). He finds himself cold when he wants to be hot, going backward when he wants to go forward, and being sluggish when he wants to be active in God's service.

He is deeply conscious of his own weaknesses. He groans under a sense of indwelling corruption. But still, despite all that, the general tendency of his heart is toward God and away from evil. He can say with David, *I consider all Your precepts concerning all things to be right, and I hate every false way* (Psalm 119:128).

When a person can say this, you have the fifth and crowning step of true repentance.

But is the picture of repentance now complete? Can I leave the subject here and go on? I cannot do it. There still remains one more thing that should never be forgotten. If I were not to mention this one thing, I might make hearts sad that God would not want made sad, and raise seeming barriers between people's souls and heaven.

True repentance, such as that which I have just described, is never alone in the heart of anyone. It always has a companion – a blessed companion. It is always accompanied by active faith in our Lord and Savior Jesus Christ. Wherever faith is, there is repentance. Wherever repentance is, there is always faith. I do not decide which comes first – whether repentance comes before faith, or faith before repentance – but I am certain enough to say that the two graces are never found separate, one from the other. Just as you cannot have the sun without light, ice without cold, fire without heat, or water without moisture, so you will never find true faith without true repentance, and you will never find true repentance without active faith. The two things will always go side by side.

Now before I go any further, let us search and examine our own hearts and see what we know about true repentance. I do not claim that the experience of all repentant people is exactly the same in every detail. I do not mean that anyone ever knows sin, mourns for sin, confesses sin, forsakes sin, or hates sin as perfectly, thoroughly, and completely as he should. But I do say that all true Christians will recognize something that they know and have felt regarding the things that I have just said.

Repentance as I have just described will generally be the experience of every true believer. Examine yourself, then, and see what you know of it in your own soul.

Be careful that you do not make a mistake about the nature of true repentance. The devil knows the value of that precious grace too well not to try to come up with imitations of it. Wherever there is good money, there will always be bad money. Wherever there is a valuable grace, the devil will put in circulation counterfeits and forgeries of that grace, and he will try to pass them off on people's souls. Make sure that you are not deceived.

Take heed that your repentance is a matter of your heart. Repentance is not a gloomy face, a self-righteous demeanor, or a list of self-imposed austerities. It is not this alone that makes up true repentance toward God. The real grace is something far deeper than a mere matter of face, clothes, traditions, and rituals. Ahab could put on sackcloth when he thought it would help him, but Ahab never repented.

Take heed that your repentance is a repentance wherein you turn to God. Roman Catholics can run to priests and confessionals when they are frightened, and Felix could tremble when he heard the apostle Paul preach (Acts 24:25), but that is not true repentance. See that your repentance leads you to God and makes you run to Him as your best Friend.

Take heed that your repentance is a repentance that results in thoroughly forsaking sin. Emotional people can cry when they hear moving sermons on Sundays, and yet return to the dance, the theater, and the opera during the week. Herod liked to hear John the Baptist preach, and *heard him gladly*, and *he did many things* (Mark 6:20). However, religious feelings are worse than worthless if they are not accompanied by practice. Mere emotional excitement, without completely breaking off from sin, is not the repentance that God approves.

Take heed, above all things, that your repentance is closely bound up with faith in the Lord Jesus Christ. Make sure that your convictions are convictions that never rest except at the foot of the cross on which Jesus Christ died. Judas Iscariot could say, *I have sinned* (Matthew 27:4), but he never turned to Jesus. Judas never looked by faith to Jesus, and therefore Judas died in his sins.

Give me that conviction of sin that makes a person flee to Christ and mourn because he realizes that by his sins he has pierced the Lord who bought him. Give me that sorrow of soul under which a person feels much about Christ, and mourns to think of the contempt he has shown to such a gracious Savior.

Going to Sinai, hearing about the Ten Commandments, looking at hell, and thinking about the terrors of damnation all might make people afraid, and it has its use, but no repentance ever lasts in which a person does not look at Calvary more than at Sinai and see in a bleeding Jesus the strongest motive for repentance. Such repentance comes down from heaven. Such repentance is planted in a person's heart by the Holy Spirit.

Section 2

Why is Repentance Necessary?

Except you repent, you will all likewise perish (Luke 13:3). This text clearly shows the necessity of repentance. The words of our Lord Jesus Christ are distinct, direct, and definite. All people, without exception, need repentance toward God. It is not only necessary for thieves, murderers, drunkards, adulterers, fornicators, and the inhabitants of prisons and of jails, but all who are born of Adam, without exception, need repentance toward God.

The queen upon her throne and the man living in poverty, the rich man in his mansion and the laborer in the warehouse, the professor at the university and the poor farmer who works hard all day long – all by nature need repentance. All are born in sin, and all must repent and be converted if they would be saved. All must have their hearts changed about sin. All must repent, as well as believe the gospel. *Except you be converted and become as little children, you will in no wise enter the kingdom of heaven* (Matthew 18:3). *Except you repent, you will all likewise perish.*

Why is there such a necessity of repentance? Why is such tremendously strong language used about this necessity? What are the reasons and the causes that repentance is so needful?

Without repentance, there is no forgiveness of sins. In saying this, I must guard myself against misunderstanding. I ask you emphatically not to misunderstand me. The tears of repentance do not wash away any sins. It is bad theology to say that they do. That is the work of the blood of Christ alone. Repentance does not make any atonement for sin. It is terrible theology to say that it does. It can do nothing of the kind. Our best repentance is a poor, imperfect thing, and needs repenting over again. Our best repentance has enough defects about it to sink us into hell. "We are counted righteous before God only for the sake of our Lord Jesus Christ, by faith, and not for our own works or deservings,"[1] not for our repentance, holiness, charity, receiving of sacraments, or anything of the kind. All this is perfectly true.

However, it is no less true that justified people are always repentant people, and that a forgiven sinner will always be someone who mourns over and hates his sins. God, in Christ, is willing to receive rebellious man and grant him peace, if only he comes to Him in Christ's name, no matter how wicked he may have been.

However, God requires, and rightly requires, the rebel

---

1   This is a quote from the Thirty-Nine Articles of the Church of England.

to throw down his weapons. The Lord Jesus Christ is ready to forgive, pardon, relieve, cleanse, wash, sanctify, and prepare for heaven, but He desires to see a person hate the sins for which he wants to be forgiven. Let some people call this legalism or bondage if they will. I take my stand on Scripture. The testimony of God's Word is plain and unmistakable. Justified people are always repentant people. Without repentance, there is no forgiveness of sins.

Without repentance, there is no real happiness in the life that now is. There might be happiness, excitement, laughter, and rejoicing, as long as health is good and money is in the bank – but these things are not solid happiness. There is a conscience in all people, and that conscience must be satisfied. As long as conscience feels that sin has not been repented of and forsaken, it will not be quiet

> There is a conscience in all people, and that conscience must be satisfied.

and will not let a person feel comfortable within. All of us have an inner man, or inner nature, unknown to the world. Our companions and friends often have no acquaintance with our inner nature. That inner man has a burden upon it, as long as sin is not repented of. Until that burden is taken off, that inner man has no real comfort.

Can you and I be comfortable when we are not in a right position with God? It is impossible. What is a person's true position? He is never in his right position until he has turned his back upon sin and turned his face toward God.

A person's house is never comfortable until all things are in order. When is the house of the inward man in order? Never – until God is king and the world is put down in the second place; never – until God is upon the throne and sin is cast down and put out of doors. You might as well expect the solar system to go on well without the sun as to expect your heart to be comfortable when God is not in His place. The great debt with God must be settled. The King must be upon His throne. Then, and not until then, will there be peace within. Without repentance, there cannot be true happiness. We must repent if we want to be happy.

Without repentance, you cannot be ready for heaven in the world that is yet to come. Heaven is a prepared place, and those who go to heaven must be a prepared people. Our hearts must be in tune for the business of heaven, or else we would find heaven itself a miserable place to live. Our minds must be in harmony with those of the inhabitants of heaven, or else the society of heaven would soon be unbearable to us.

I would gladly help everyone to heaven who is reading this, but I want you to know that if you went there with an unrepentant heart, heaven would not be heaven to your soul. What could you possibly do in heaven if you got there with a heart that loves sin? To which of the saints would you speak? By whose side would you sit down? Surely the music of the angels of God would not be sweet to the heart of him who cannot tolerate saints upon earth and who never praised the Lamb for His redeeming love! Certainly the company of patriarchs, apostles, and prophets would not be joy to that person who will not read his Bible now and who does not care to know what the apostles and prophets wrote.

No! No! There can be no happiness in heaven if we get there with an unrepentant heart. The fish is not happy when it is out of water. The bird is not happy when it is confined in a cage. Why? They are all out of their proper element and natural environment. In the same way, an unconverted, unrepentant person would not be happy if he got to heaven without a heart changed by the Holy Spirit. He would be a creature out of his proper element. He would have no ability to enjoy his holy abode. Without a repentant heart, he is not suitable for the *inheritance of the saints in light* (Colossians 1:12). We must repent if we want to go to heaven.

I implore you by the mercies of God to take to heart what I have just been saying. Consider it thoroughly. You live in a world of cheating, fraud, and deception. Do not let anyone deceive you about the necessity of repentance. Oh, that professing Christians would see, know, and feel the necessity, the absolute necessity, of true repentance toward God more than they do!

There are many things that are not necessary. Riches are not necessary. Health is not necessary. Fine clothes are not necessary. Distinguished friends are not necessary. The favor of the world is not necessary. Talents and education are not necessary. Millions of people have reached heaven without these things. Thousands are reaching heaven every year without them. However, no one ever reached heaven without *repentance toward God, and faith toward our Lord Jesus Christ* (Acts 20:21).

Do not ever let anyone convince you that any religion

that does not have repentance toward God in a most prominent place deserves to be called the gospel. A gospel indeed! That is no gospel in which repentance is not a primary thing. A gospel! It is the gospel of man, but not of God. A gospel! It comes from earth, but not from heaven. A gospel! It is not the gospel at all; it is contrary to the gospel! As long as you cling to your sins and want to keep your sins, you can talk as you want to about the gospel, but your sins are not forgiven.

You can call that legalism if you want to. If you want to, you can say, "I hope it will be all right for me at the end. God is merciful. God is love. Christ has died. I hope I will go to heaven." No! I tell you, it is not all right. It will never be all right like that. You are trampling underfoot the blood of atonement (Hebrews 10:29). You have as yet no part or lot in Christ (Acts 8:21). As long as you do not repent of sin, the gospel of our Lord Jesus Christ is no gospel to your soul. Christ is a Savior from sin, not a Savior for man in sin. If a man wants to keep his sins, the day will come when that merciful Savior will say to him, *Depart from Me, you worker of iniquity! Depart into everlasting fire, prepared for the devil and his angels* (Matthew 25:41).

Do not ever let anyone deceive you into thinking that you can be happy in this world without repentance. Oh, no! You can laugh and dance, go on vacations, tell good jokes, sing good songs, and say, "Hurrah! There are good times ahead!" – but none of this proves that you are happy. As long as you do not break with sin, you will never be truly happy.

Thousands of people go on like this for a little while,

and they seem happy to others, yet they carry around in their hearts a hidden sorrow. When they are alone, they are miserable. When they are not in lighthearted company, they are downcast. Their conscience makes cowards of them. They do not like being by themselves. They hate quiet thinking. They must constantly have some new excitement. Every year they must have more. Just as a drug addict needs larger and larger doses, so the person who seeks happiness in anything except in God needs greater excitement every year that he lives, and even then he is never really happy.

Yes – and worse than that, the longer you continue without repentance, the more unhappy your heart will be. When old age creeps over you and grey hairs appear upon your head – when you are unable to go where you once went and take pleasure in what you once took pleasure – then your wretchedness and misery will break in upon you like an armed man. The more unrepentant a person is, the more miserable he becomes.

> The longer you continue without repentance, the more unhappy your heart will be.

Have you ever heard of the great clock of St. Paul's Cathedral in London? At noon, during the roar of business, when carriages, carts, wagons, and omnibuses go rolling through the streets, many people never hear that great clock strike unless they live very near it. But when the work of the day is over and the roar of business has passed away, when people have gone to sleep and silence reigns in London – then at twelve, at one, at two, at three, at four – the sound of that clock can be heard for miles around. Twelve! One! Two! Three! Four! How that clock is heard by many sleepless people!

That clock is just like the conscience of the unrepentant person. While he has health and strength and goes on in the whirl of business, he will not hear his conscience. He drowns and silences its voice by plunging into the world. He will not allow the inner man to speak to him. But the day will come when his conscience will be heard whether he likes it or not. The day will come when its voice will sound in his ears and pierce him like a sword. The time will come when he must withdraw from the world, lie down on the sickbed, and look death in the face. Then the clock of conscience, that solemn clock, will sound in his heart, and if he has not repented, it will bring agony and misery to his soul. Write it down in the tablets of your heart: without repentance, there is no peace!

Above all, let no one cause you to think that there is a possibility of reaching heaven without repentance toward God. We all want to go to heaven. Someone would rightly be described as insane if he said that he wanted to go to hell. But never let it be forgotten that no one goes to heaven except those whom the Holy Spirit has prepared for it.

I make my solemn protest against those modern delusions that all people will end up in heaven, that it does not matter how you live, that it does not matter whether you are holy or unholy, or that whether you are godless or God-fearing, everyone will get to heaven. I cannot find such teaching in the Bible. The Bible firmly contradicts it. Mo matter how this new idea might be misleadingly explained, and no matter how it might seem to be defended, it cannot stand the test of the Word of God. No! Let God be true, and every man a liar (Romans 3:4).

Heaven is not such a place as some seem to imagine. The inhabitants of heaven are not such a mixed multitude as many try to believe. They are all of one heart and one mind. Heaven is the place to which God's people will go, but for those who are unrepentant and unbelieving and will not come to Christ, the Bible says plainly and unmistakably that there remains nothing for them but hell.

It is a somber thought that an unrepentant person is unfit for heaven. He could not be happy in heaven even if he got there. I remember hearing of a clergyman who was traveling by coach. He sat by the coachman's side. The coachman was one of those unhappy people who think that nothing is to be done without swearing. He was cursing, swearing, blaspheming, and taking God's name in vain, for many long miles. On he drove, flying into a rage, beating his horses, and cursing and swearing again. Such were the coachman's ways.

At last the clergyman said to him quietly, "Coachman, I am very afraid for you."

"Sir," said the coachman, "what should you be afraid of? Everything is going well. We are not likely to have any trouble."

"Coachman," said the clergyman, "I am very afraid for you because I cannot imagine what you would do in heaven if you got there. There will be no cursing in heaven. There will be no swearing in heaven. There will be no angry tempers in heaven. There will be no horses to beat in heaven. Coachman, I cannot imagine what you would do in heaven."

"Oh," said the coachman, "that is your opinion," and no more was said. Years passed by. The day came when someone told this same clergyman that a sick man, a stranger, desired to see him. He had come into the town, he said, because he wanted to die there. The clergyman went to see him. He entered a room and found a dying man whose face he did not know. "Sir," said the dying man, "do you not remember me?"

"No," said the clergyman, "I do not."

"Sir," said the man, "I remember you. I am that coachman to whom, many years ago, you said, 'Coachman, I am afraid for you because I do not know what you would do if you got to heaven.' Sir, those words laid hold upon me. I realized that I was not prepared to die. Those words worked, and worked, and worked in my heart, and I did not rest until I had repented of sin, fled to Christ, found peace in Him, and became a new man. And now, by the grace of God, I trust I am prepared to meet my Maker and am fit for the inheritance of the saints in light."

Once more I ask you to remember that without repentance toward God, you cannot be ready for heaven. It would be painful for an unrepentant person to be there. It would be no mercy to him. He would not be happy. He could not be happy. There could be no enjoyment in heaven for someone who got there without a heart that hates sin and loves God.

I expect to see many wonders at the last day. I

expect to see some at the right hand of the Lord Jesus Christ whom I once feared I would see upon the left. I expect to see some at the left hand whom I thought were good Christians and expected to see at the right. But there is one thing I am sure I will not see: I will not see one single unrepentant person at the right hand of Jesus Christ.

I will see Abraham there, who said, *I am dust and ashes* (Genesis 18:27). I will see Jacob there, who said, *I am not worthy of the least of all Your mercies* (Genesis 32:10). I will see Job there, who said, *I am vile* (Job 40:4). I will see David there, who said, *I was shaped in iniquity; in sin did my mother conceive me* (Psalm 51:5). I will see Isaiah there, who said, *I am a man of unclean lips* (Isaiah 6:5). I will see Paul there, who said, *I am the chief of sinners* (1 Timothy 1:15).

> I will not see one single unrepentant person at the right hand of Jesus Christ.

I will see the martyr John Bradford there, who often signed the end of his letters with "That wretched sinner, that miserable sinner, John Bradford." This is that same John Bradford who, whenever he saw a man going to be hanged, said, "There goes John Bradford, but for the grace of God." I will see James Ussher there, whose last words were "Pardon my many sins, especially my sins of omission." I will see William Grimshaw there, whose last words were "Here goes an unprofitable servant."

But they will all be of one heart, one mind, and one experience. They will all have hated sin. They will all have mourned for sin. They will all have confessed sin. They will all have forsaken sin. They will all have repented, as well as believed – repented toward God, as well as believed in Jesus Christ. They will all say with one voice, *What has God wrought!* (Numbers 23:23). They will all say, "By the grace of God I am where I am," as well as *By the grace of God I am what I am* (1 Corinthians 15:10).

Section 3

What is There to Lead a Person to Repent?

Ⅰ now come to the third and last thing that I promised to address. *I will consider the encouragements to repentance. What is there to lead a person to repent?*

I feel it is very important to say something about this. I know that many difficulties appear before us when the subject of repentance is brought up. I know how slow people are to give up sin. You might as well tell them to cut off a right hand, pluck out a right eye, or cut off a right foot as to tell them to part with their favorite sins.

I know the strength of old habits and the early ways of thinking about Christianity. They start out like cobwebs, but end up as iron chains. I know the power of pride and the fear of man that *brings a snare* (Proverbs 29:25). I know the dislike there is in people to being thought of as a saint and supposed to care about

Christianity. I know that hundreds and thousands would never run from going to war who cannot bear to be laughed at and thought ridiculous because they care about their souls. I know, too, the hatred of our great enemy, the devil. Will he part with his "lawful captives" without a conflict (Isaiah 49:24)? Never! Will he give up his prey without a fight? Never!

I once saw a lion being fed at a zoo. I saw his meal thrown down before him. I saw the keeper try to take that meal away. I remember the lion's roar, his spring, and his struggle to retain his food. I remember, too, the roaring lion that walks about, *seeking whom he may devour* (1 Peter 5:8). Will he give up a man or a woman without a struggle, and let him repent? Never, never, never! Man needs many encouragements to make him repent.

However, there are encouragements – great, broad, wide, full, and free. There are things in the Word of God that should strengthen every heart and stir up everyone to repent without delay. I want to bring these things before you now. I do not want even one person to say, "This cannot be done; it is impossible." I want all who read this to say, "There is hope; there is hope! There is an open door! It is possible! This can be done! By the grace of God, a person can repent!"

> It is possible! This can be done! By the grace of God, a person can repent!

Hear what a gracious Savior the Lord Jesus Christ is. I place Him first and foremost as the greatest argument to encourage a person to repent. I say to every doubting soul, "Look at Christ; think of Christ." *He is able to save to the uttermost all who come unto God by Him* (Hebrews 7:25). He is one anointed *a Prince and a Savior*, to give repentance as well as forgiveness of sins (Acts 5:31). He is one who came *to seek and to save that which was lost* (Luke 19:10). He is one who said, *I came not to call the righteous, but sinners to repentance* (Luke 5:32). He is one who cries, *Come unto Me, all you who labor and are heavy laden, and I will give you rest* (Matthew 11:28). He is one who has pledged His royal word: *Him who comes unto Me, I will never cast out* (John 6:37). He it is of whom it is written, *As many as received Him, to them gave He power to become the sons of God, even to those who believe on His name* (John 1:12).

I answer all doubts, questions, difficulties, objections, and fears with this simple argument. I say to everyone who needs encouragement: "Look at Christ; think of Christ." Consider Jesus Christ, the Lord, and then doubt about repentance no more.

Hear what glorious promises the Word of God contains. It is written, *Whoever confesses and forsakes his sins will find mercy* (Proverbs 28:13). The Bible says, *If we confess our sins, He is faithful and just to forgive us our sins, and to cleanse us from all unrighteousness* (1 John 1:9). God's Word also says, *Blessed are the poor in spirit, for theirs is the kingdom of God. Blessed are those who mourn, for they will be comforted. . . . Blessed are those who hunger and thirst after righteousness, for they will be filled* (Matthew 5:3-4, 6). Surely these promises are encouragements. Again I say, doubt about repentance no more.

Hear what gracious declarations the Word of God contains. *When the wicked man turns away from his wickedness that he has committed, and does that which is lawful and right, he will save his soul alive* (Ezekiel 18:27). *The sacrifices of God are a broken spirit: a broken and a contrite heart, O God, You will not despise* (Psalm 51:17). God is *not willing that any should perish, but that all should come to repentance* (2 Peter 3:9). *As I live, says the Lord God, I have no pleasure in the death of the wicked. . . . Turn! Turn! Why will you die?* (Ezekiel 33:11). *There is joy in the presence of the angels of God over one sinner that repents* (Luke 15:10). Certainly if any words can be encouraging, these words are! Again I say, doubt about repentance no more.

Hear what marvelous parables our Lord Jesus spoke upon this subject. *Two men went up to the temple to pray, one a Pharisee and the other a tax collector. The Pharisee took his stand and was praying like this: "God, I thank You that I'm not like other people – greedy, unrighteous, adulterers, or even like this tax collector. I fast twice a week; I give a tenth of everything I get." But the tax collector, standing far off, would not even raise his eyes to heaven but kept striking his chest and saying, "God, turn Your wrath from me – a sinner!" I tell you, this one went down to his house justified rather than the other; because everyone who exalts himself will be humbled, but the one who humbles himself will be exalted.* (Luke 18:10-14)

Hear also that other marvelous parable – the parable of the prodigal son.

A man had two sons. The younger of them said to his father, "Father, give me the share of the estate I have coming to me." So he distributed the assets to them. Not many days later, the younger son gathered together all he had and traveled to a distant country, where he squandered his estate in foolish living. After he had spent everything, a severe famine struck that country, and he had nothing. Then he went to work for one of the citizens of that country, who sent him into his fields to feed pigs. He longed to eat his fill from the carob pods the pigs were eating, but no one would give him any.

When he came to his senses, he said, "How many of my father's hired hands have more than enough food, and here I am dying of hunger! I'll get up, go to my father, and say to him, Father, I have sinned against heaven and in your sight. I'm no longer worthy to be called your son. Make me like one of your hired hands."

So he got up and went to his father. But while the son was still a long way off, his father saw him and was filled with compassion. He ran, threw his arms around his neck, and kissed him. The son said to him, "Father, I have sinned against heaven and in your sight. I'm no longer worthy to be called your son."

But the father told his servants, "Quick! Bring out the best robe and put it on him; put a ring on his finger and sandals on his feet. Then bring the fattened calf and slaughter it, and let's celebrate with a feast, because this son of mine was dead and is alive again; he was lost and is found!" So they began to celebrate. (Luke 15:11-24)

Surely these are mighty encouragements to repentance. Again I say, doubt about repentance no more.

Hear what wonderful examples there are in the Word of God of God's mercy and kindness to repentant people. Read the story of David. What sin can be greater than David's sin? However, when David turned to the Lord, and said, *I have sinned against the Lord*, the answer came, *The Lord has put away your sin* (2 Samuel 12:13).

Read the story of Manasseh. What wickedness could have been greater than his? He killed his own children. He turned his back upon his father's God. He placed idols in the temple. Yet when Manasseh was in prison and humbled himself and prayed to the Lord, the Lord heard his prayer and brought him out of captivity (2 Chronicles 33:1-19).

Read the history of Peter. What apostasy could be greater than his? He denied his Master three times with an oath! Yet when Peter wept and mourned for his sin, there was mercy even for Peter, and repentant Peter was restored to his Master's favor (Mark 16:7).

Read the story of the repentant thief. What case could be more desperate than his? He was a dying man on the brink of hell. Yet when he said to Jesus, *Lord, remember me when You come into Your kingdom*, at once the marvelous answer came, *Verily I say unto you, Today you will be with Me in paradise* (Luke 23:39-43).

What greater encouragement to repentance can be imagined or conceived? Why are all these cases recorded for our learning? They are intended to lead people to repentance. They are all patterns of God's long-suffering, mercy, and willingness to receive repentant sinners. They are proof of what God's grace can do. They are a cloud of witnesses, proving that it is worthwhile for a person to repent, that there is encouragement for people to turn to God, and that those who continue still in their sins are completely without excuse. *The goodness of God leads you to repentance* (Romans 2:4).

I remember hearing of a mother whose daughter ran away from her and lived a life of sin. For a long time, no one knew where she was, yet that daughter came back and was restored. She truly repented. She learned to mourn for sin. She turned to Christ and believed in Him. Old things passed away, and all things became new (2 Corinthians 5:17).

Her mother was asked one day to tell what she had done to bring her daughter back. What method had she used? What steps had she taken? Her reply was very remarkable. She said, "I prayed for her night and day." But that was not all. She went on to say, "I never went to bed at night without leaving my front door unlocked. I thought that if my daughter came back some night

The door of mercy is set wide open.

when I was in bed, she would never be able to say that she found the door locked. She would never be able to say that she came to her mother's home but could not get in." And that is how it happened. Her daughter came back one night, tried the door, and found the door open. She went in at once, to go out and sin no more. That open door was the saving of her soul.

That open door is a beautiful illustration of the

heart of God toward sinners! The door of mercy is set wide open. The door is not yet locked. The door can be opened. God's heart is full of love. God's heart is full of compassion. Whoever and whatever a person might have been, at midnight or at any time, whenever he returns to God, he will find God willing to receive him, ready to pardon him, and glad to have him at home. All things are ready. Whoever desires to enter can come in.

Out of all the millions who have turned to God and repented, whoever repented of repentance? I answer boldly, "Not one!" Thousands every year repent of foolishness and unbelief. Thousands mourn over wasted time or time spent in a wrong way. Thousands regret their drunkenness, gambling, immorality, profanity, idleness, and neglected opportunities. But no one has ever risen up and declared to the world that he repents of repenting and turning toward God. The steps in the narrow way of life are all in one direction. You will never see in the narrow way the step of one who turned back because the narrow way was not good.

> No one has ever risen up and declared to the world that he repents of repenting and turning toward God.

I remember reading of a remarkable event that occurred in a place of worship where a Puritan minister, Mr. Doolittle, was preaching a couple hundred years ago. Just as he was about to begin his sermon, he saw a young man, a stranger, enter his church. He guessed by the young man's manner that he was concerned about his soul, yet undecided about Christianity. He took an unusual course with him. He tried an interesting experiment, but God blessed it to the young man's soul.

Before Mr. Doolittle read his text, he turned to an old Christian whom he saw on one side of his church. He addressed him by name, and asked him, "Brother, do you repent of having served God?" The old Christian stood up boldly before the congregation and said, "Sir, I have served the Lord from my youth, and He has never done me anything but good."

Mr. Doolittle turned to the left, where he saw another Christian, and addressed him in the same way. "Brother," he said, calling him by his name, "do you repent of having served Christ?" That man also stood up boldly before the congregation and said, "Sir, I was never truly happy until I took up the cross and served the Lord Jesus Christ."

Then Mr. Doolittle turned to the young man and said, "Young man, will you repent? Young man, will you take up the cross? Young man, will you this day begin to serve Christ?" God sent power with these words. The young man stood up before the congregation and said in a humble tone, "Yes, sir. I will." That very day was the beginning of eternal life in the young man's soul.

We can depend upon it that the two answers that Mr. Doolittle got that day from the two older men tell the experience of all true Christians. We can be quite sure that no one ever repents of repentance. No one was ever sorry that he served the Lord. No one ever said at the end of his days, "I have read my Bible too much. I have thought of God too much. I have prayed too much. I have been too concerned about my soul."

Oh, no! The people of God would always say, "If I had my life to live over again, I would walk far more closely with God than I have done. I am sorry that I have not served God better, but I am not sorry that I have served Him. The way of Christ might have its cross, but it is a way of pleasantness and a path of peace."

Surely that fact alone speaks volumes. It is a fact that clinches every argument that I have already advanced. Surely it is worthwhile for a person to repent. There are encouragements. The unrepentant person is without excuse.

Conclusion

I have now brought before my readers the three points that I introduced at the beginning. I have shown you the nature of repentance toward God, the necessity of repentance, and the encouragements to repentance. I will conclude with a few words of practical and tender application to the souls of all who read this.

My first word will be a word of warning. I offer a tender warning to every unrepentant soul into whose hands this volume may fall. I cannot for a moment suppose that all who read its pages are truly repentant toward God and are active believers in Jesus Christ. I dare not think that is true. I cannot think it. My first word will be a word of warning – tender, affectionate warning – to all unrepentant and unconverted people who may happen to read this.

What stronger warning can I give you than that which my text contains? What words can I use that could be more solemn and more heart-searching than the words of my Lord and Master: *Except you repent, you will all likewise perish!* Yes! You who are reading this and know that you are not yet at peace with God, you who are hesitating, lingering, and undecided regarding Christ – you are the one to whom the words of the text should come with power: *Except you repent, you, even you, will perish!*

Oh, think what dreadful words these are! Who can measure out the full amount of what they contain? *Will perish!* Perish in body, perish in soul, and perish miserably at last in hell! I dare not attempt to paint the horrors of that thought. The worm that never dies, the fire that is not quenched (Mark 9:48), the blackness of darkness forever (Jude 1:13), the hopeless prison, the bottomless pit (Revelation 9:1-2), the lake that burns with fire and brimstone (Revelation 21:8) –are all only feeble descriptions of the reality of hell.

It is to this hell that all unrepentant people are daily traveling! Yes – from churches and chapels, from rich mansions and poor cottages, from the midst of knowledge, wealth, and respectability – all who will not repent are certainly traveling toward hell. *Except you repent, you will all likewise perish!*

Think how great your danger is! Where are your sins, your many sins? You know you are a sinner. You must be aware of it. It is foolish to pretend you have not committed any sins. Where are your sins if you have not yet repented, if you have not yet mourned for sin, if you have never confessed sin, if you have never fled to Christ, and if you have never found pardon through Christ's blood? Oh, take heed to yourself. The pit of hell opens her mouth for you (Isaiah 5:14). The devil is saying of you, "He will be mine!" Take heed to yourself.

Remember the words of the text: *Except you repent, you will all likewise perish!* They are not my words, but they are Christ's words. Christ says it. Christ, the merciful one, Christ, the gracious one, says, *Except you repent, you will likewise perish!*

Think again of your guilt! Yes, I say, purposely think of your guilt. It is guilt when a person does not repent. We are responsible and accountable to God for repentance. It is foolish to say we are not. What does Paul say to the Athenians? *God commands all people everywhere to repent* (Acts 17:30). What does our Lord say of Chorazin and Bethsaida? Why were they so guilty? Why was their position in hell to be so intolerable? Because they would not repent and believe (Luke 10:13). It is the direct testimony of the Son of God that the unrepentant person who has been called to repentance and has refused to obey the call is more guilty than the person who has never been urged to repent.

> When your last hour comes, what can all the gold in the world do for you if you die without having repented?

Think of the foolishness of remaining an unrepentant person! Yes, I say it is foolish. The world you cling to is already melting beneath your feet. What will money do for you in the life to come? What will your gold be worth to you a hundred years from now? When your last hour comes, what can all the gold in the world do for you if you die without having repented? You might live for the world now. You strive hard and furiously to be successful in business. You compass sea and land to add acre to acre or to accumulate riches in the stock market. You do all you can to get money, to acquire riches, to make yourself comfortable, to have pleasure, and to leave something for your wife and children when you die. But remember that if you do not have the grace of God and true repentance, you are a poor man in the sight of God.

I will never forget the effect produced upon my own mind when I read some years ago of that fearful shipwreck, the loss of the *Central America* – a great steamer that was lost on the voyage from Havana to New York. That steamer was bringing home from California three or four hundred gold diggers. They had all got their gold and were coming home, planning to spend their latter days in ease in their own country. But man proposes, and God disposes (Proverbs 16:9).

About twenty-four hours after the *Central America* left Havana, a mighty storm arose. Three or four heavy waves struck the ship in succession and seriously damaged her. The engines became disabled and useless, and she was tossed around by the wild sea. She sprung a leak, and despite every effort, the ship began to fill with water.

After a while, when all on board had pumped and baled and baled and pumped until they were exhausted, it became plain that the *Central America*, with her three or four hundred passengers and all her crew, was likely to go down into the deep, deep sea, carrying nearly all on board with her. The crew launched the only boats they had. They placed the women passengers in these boats with just a sufficient number of sailors to manage them. All honor be to them for their kind regard to the weak and defenseless at a time like that!

The boats were rowed away from the vessel, but there were two or three hundred people left behind, many of them gold diggers, when the *Central America* went down.

One man who left the ship in one of the last boats that took the women described what he saw in the cabin of the steamer when all hope was gone and the great ship was about to go down. People took out their gold. One man, holding his leather bag that contained his long-worked-for accumulations, yelled, "Here – whoever wants it can take it! It is of no more use to me. The ship is going down. Take it whoever will." Others took out their gold and scattered it all over. "There," they said, "take it – take it whoever will! We are all going down. There is no more chance for us. The gold will do us no good!"

Oh, what a comment that is on the truly valueless nature of riches when a person draws near to God! *Riches profit not in the day of wrath: but righteousness delivers from death* (Proverbs 11:4). Think of your foolishness – your foolishness as well as your danger, your foolishness as well as your guilt – if you will cling to your sins. Think of your foolishness if you will not hear the warning that I give you today. In my Master's name, I say to you once more, *Except you repent,* you, even you who are reading this, *you will likewise perish!*

My second word of application will be an invitation to all who feel their sins and desire to repent,

and yet do not know what to do. I give it broadly and fully to all who ask me, "What should I do right now if I am to take your advice?" I answer that question without any hesitation. I say to you, in my Master's name, "Repent, repent, repent this very day. Repent without delay."

I have no difficulty in saying this. I cannot agree with those who say that unconverted people should not be told to repent or pray. I find the apostle Peter saying to Simon Magus, *Repent of this your wickedness.* I find him saying, *Pray to the Lord that the intent of your heart may be forgiven you* (Acts 8:22). I am content to follow in Peter's trail.

I say the same to everyone who is concerned about his soul. I say, "Repent, repent, repent without delay." The time will soon come when you must have this settled, if you ever will. Why not this very day? Why not now? Sermon-hearing cannot go on forever. Going to churches and chapels must have an end. Liking this minister and that minister, belonging to this church and that chapel, holding these views and those views, thinking this preacher is sound and that preacher is unsound – is not enough to save a soul. A person must act, as well as think, if he intends to go to heaven. A person must break off from his sins and flee to the Lord Jesus if he does not want to be damned. A person must come out from the world and take up the cross. A person must be deliberate and repent and believe. A person must

> A person must act, as well as think, if he intends to go to heaven.

36

fly his flag and be on the Lord Jesus Christ's side if he intends to be saved. Why not begin all this today? Repent, repent, repent without delay!

Do you ask me again what you should do? Go, I tell you, and cry to the Lord Jesus Christ this very moment. Go and pour out your heart before Him. Go and tell Him what you are, and tell Him what you desire. Tell Him you are a sinner; He will not be ashamed of you. Tell Him you want to be saved; He will hear you. Tell Him you are a poor, weak creature; He will listen to you. Tell Him you do not know what to do or how to repent; He will give you His grace. He will pour out His Spirit upon you. He will hear you. He will grant your prayer. He will save your soul. There is enough in Christ, and more than enough, for all the needs of all the world, for all the needs of every heart that is unconverted, unsanctified, unbelieving, unrepentant, and unrenewed.

"What is your hope?" a man asked a poor Welsh boy who could not speak much English and was found dying in an inn one day. "What is your hope about your soul?" What was his reply? He turned to the questioner and said to him in broken English, "Jesus Christ is plenty for everybody! Jesus Christ is plenty for everybody!" There is a wealth of truth in those words. It was also well said by a navigator who died in the Lord, "Tell them all, tell everyone you meet – Christ is for everyone! Jesus Christ is for everyone!" Go to the Savior this day and tell Him the needs of your soul. Go to Him in the words of that beautiful hymn:

Just as I am, without one plea,
　　But that Your blood was shed for me,
And that You bid me come to Thee,
　　O Lamb of God, I come!

Just as I am, and waiting not
　　To rid my soul of one dark blot,
To Thee, whose blood can cleanse each spot –
　　O Lamb of God, I come![2]

Go to the Lord Jesus in that spirit, and He will receive you. He will not refuse you. He will not despise you. He will grant you pardon, peace, and everlasting life, and He will give you the grace of the Holy Spirit.

Do you ask me if there is anything else you should do? Yes! Go and be determined to break off from every known sin. Let those who will call such advice legalism, but I hope I will never hold back from giving it. It can never be right to sit still in wickedness. It can never be wrong to say with Isaiah, *Cease to do evil* (Isaiah 1:16).

Whatever your sins are, resolve, by God's help, that you will be a different person and will leave and break off from your sins. Whether it is drinking, or swearing, or an angry temper, or lying, or cheating, or covetousness, or immorality – whatever your sins and transgressions, determine, by God's grace, that you will break off immediately from them. Give them up without delay. Turn from them, by God's help, for the rest of your days. Cast them from you, for they are as a serpent that will bite you to death. Throw them

---

2　This is from the hymn "Just as I Am" by Charlotte Elliott.

from you, for they are as useless lumber that will sink the ship down to destruction. Cast away your besetting sin that entangles you (Hebrews 12:1). Give it up. Turn from it. Break it off. By God's help, resolve that in that matter you will sin no more.

I think it is possible, though, that someone reading this might be ashamed of repentance. I urge you to cast away such shame for ever. Never be ashamed of repentance toward God. You can be ashamed of sin. A person should be ashamed of lying, swearing, drunkenness, gambling, and immorality, but of repentance, prayer, faith in Christ, seeking God, and caring for your soul – never, never, as long as you live – never be ashamed of such things as these.

I remember, long ago, when I learned something that gave me some idea of what the fear of man can do. I was attending a dying man who had been a sergeant in the army. He had ruined his health by drinking alcohol. He had been careless and thoughtless about his soul. He told me upon his deathbed that when he first began to pray, he was so ashamed of his wife knowing it that when he went upstairs to pray, he would take his shoes off and sneak up in his socks so that his wife would not know how he was spending his time. I am afraid there are many like him! Do not be one of them. Whatever you are ashamed of, never be ashamed of seeking God.

I think it might be possible that some reader is afraid to repent. You think you are so bad and unworthy that Christ will not have you. I urge you once more to cast away such fear forever. Never, never be afraid to repent. The Lord Jesus Christ is very gracious. He will not break the bruised reed, nor quench the smoking flax (Matthew 12:20). Do not be afraid to draw near to Him. There is a confessional ready for you. You do not need one made by man. The throne of grace is the true confessional. There is a Priest ready for you. You do not need any ordained man – no priest, no bishop, no minister – to stand between you and God. The Lord Jesus is the true High Priest. There is none as wise and loving as He. None but He can give you absolution and send you away with a light heart and in perfect peace. Oh, take the invitation I bring to you. Fear nothing. Christ is not *an austere man* (Luke 19:21). He despises none (Job 36:5). Arise today and flee to Him. Go to Christ and repent now without delay.

My last word of application will be an exhortation to all who have known what repentance is by experience. I address it to all who have, by God's grace, known their sins, sorrowed for their sins, confessed their sins, given up their sins, and found peace in the blood of Jesus Christ. I say to you: "Keep up your repentance!" Let it be a habit of mind you watch over to the last day of your life. Let it be a fire you never allow to burn low or to become dull. If you love life, keep up your repentance.

I do not want you to make a Savior of repentance or to turn it into a bondage for your soul. I do not ask you to measure the degree of your justification by your repentance or to think that your sins are not forgiven because your repentance is imperfect. Justification is one thing, and repentance is another. You must not confuse things that are different. It is only faith that justifies. It is only faith that lays hold of Christ, but you must keep a jealous watch over your repentance. Keep it up. Keep it up, and do not let the fire burn low.

Whenever you find your soul slipping – whenever you feel slow, sluggish, heavy, cold, and careless about little sins – look to your own heart then, and take heed lest you fall (1 Corinthians 10:12). Say to your soul, "Oh, my soul, what are you doing? Have you forgotten David's fall? Have you forgotten Peter's backsliding? Have you forgotten David's subsequent misery? Have you forgotten Peter's tears? Awake, O my soul. Awake once more." Pour on fuel and make the fire burn bright. Return again to your God. Let your repentance once more be active and alive. Let your repentance be repented over again. How few are the hours in a Christian's best days when he does not make work for repentance!

Keep up your repentance until the last day of your life. There will always be sins to lament and faults to confess. Take them daily to the Lord Jesus Christ, and obtain from Him daily supplies of mercy and grace. Make confession daily to the great High Priest, and receive from Him daily absolution. Feed daily on the Passover Lamb, but never forget that it was to be eaten *with bitter herbs* (Exodus 12:8).

"Sir," said a young man to Philip Henry, "how long should a person go on repenting?" What did old Philip Henry reply? "Sir, I hope to carry my repentance to the very gates of heaven. Every day I find I am a sinner, and every day I need to repent. I intend to carry my repentance, by God's help, up to the very gates of heaven."

May this be our belief and our practice – your

theology and my theology! May repentance toward God and faith toward our Lord Jesus Christ (Acts 20:21) be the two great pillars before the temple of our religion (2 Chronicles 3:17), the cornerstones in our system of Christianity! May the two never be separated! May we, while we repent, believe; and while we believe, may we repent! May repentance and faith, faith and repentance, always be uppermost and foremost, and the chief and main articles in the creed of our souls!

J. C. Ryle – A Brief Biography

John Charles Ryle was born into a wealthy, affluent, socially elite family on May 10, 1816 – the first-born son of John Ryle, a banker, and his wife Susanna (Wirksworth) Ryle. As the firstborn, John lived a privileged life and was set to inherit all of his father's estate and pursue a career in Parliament. His future promised to be planned and comfortable with no material needs.

J. C. Ryle attended a private school and then earned academic scholarships to Eton (1828) and the University of Oxford (1834), but he excelled in sports. He particularly made his mark in rowing and cricket. Though his pursuit of sports was short lived, he claimed that they gave him leadership gifts. "It gave me a power of commanding, managing, organizing and directing, seeing through men's capabilities and using every man in the post to which he was best suited, bearing and forbearing, keeping men around me in good temper, which I have found of infinite use on lots of occasions in life, though in very different matters."

In 1837, before graduation, Ryle contracted a serious chest infection, which caused him to turn to the Bible and prayer for the first time in over fourteen years. One Sunday he entered church late as Ephesians 2:8 was being read – slowly, phrase by phrase. John felt the Lord was speaking to him personally, and he claims to have been converted at that moment through the Word without any commentary or sermon.

His biographer wrote, "He came under conviction, was converted, and from that moment to the last recorded syllable of this life, no doubt ever lingered in John's mind that the Word of God was living and powerful, sharper than any two-edged sword."

After graduation from Oxford, John went to London to study law for his career in politics, but in 1841, his father's bank crashed. That was the end of the career in politics, for he had no funding to continue.

In later years, John wrote, "We got up one summer's morning with all the world before us as usual, and went to bed that same night completely and entirely ruined. The immediate consequences were bitter and painful in the extreme, and humiliating to the utmost degree."

And at another time, he said, "The plain fact was there was no one of the family whom it touched more than it did me. My father and mother were no longer young and in the downhill of life; my brothers and sisters, of course, never expected to live at Henbury (the family home) and naturally never thought of it as their house after a certain time. I, on the contrary, as the eldest son, twenty-five, with all the world before me, lost everything, and saw the whole future of my life turned upside down and thrown into confusion."

After this financial ruin from abundance, Ryle was a commoner – all in a day. For the first time in his life, he needed a job. His education qualified him for the clergy, so with his Oxford degree, he was ordained and entered the ministry of the Church of England. He proceeded in a totally different direction with his first assignment in the ministry at Exbury in Hampshire, but it was a rural area riddled with disease. His recurring lung infection made a difficult couple of years until he was transferred to St. Thomas in Winchester. With his commanding presence, passionately held principles, and warm disposition, John's congregation grew so large and strong it needed different accommodations.

Ryle accepted a position at that time in Helmington, Suffolk, where he had much time to read theologians like Wesley, Bunyan, Knox, Calvin, and Luther. He was a contemporary of Charles Spurgeon, Dwight Moody, George Mueller, and Hudson Taylor. He lived in the age of Dickens, Darwin, and the American Civil War. All of these influenced Ryle's understanding and theology.

His writing career began from the tragedy of the Great Yarmouth suspension bridge. On May 9, 1845, a large crowd gathered for the official grand opening festivities, but the bridge collapsed and more than a hundred people plunged into the water and drowned. The incident shocked the whole country but it led Ryle to write his first tract. He spoke of life's uncertainties and God's sure provision of salvation through Jesus Christ. Thousands of copies were sold.

That same year, he married Matilda Plumptre, but she died after only two years, leaving him with an infant daughter. In 1850, he married Jessie Walker, but she had a lingering sickness, which caused Ryle to care for her and their growing family (three sons and another daughter) for ten years until she died. In 1861, he was transferred to Stradbroke, Suffolk, where he married Henrietta Clowes.

Stradbroke, Suffolk, was Ryle's last parish, and he gained a reputation for his straightforward preaching and evangelism. Besides his travelling and preaching, he spent time writing. He wrote more than 300 pamphlets, tracts, and books. His books include *Expository Thoughts on the Gospels* (7 Volumes, 1856-1869), *Principles for Churchmen* (1884), *Home Truths, Knots Untied, Old Paths,* and *Holiness.*

His *Christian Leaders of the Eighteenth Century* (1869) is described as having "short, pithy sentences, compelling logic and penetrating insight into spiritual power." This seems to be the case with most of his writing as he preached and wrote with five main guidelines: (1) Have a clear view of the subject, (2) Use simple words, (3) Use a simple style of composition, (4) Be direct, and (5) Use plenty of anecdotes and illustrations.

In all of his success with writing, he used the royalties to pay his father's debts. He may have felt indebted to that financial ruin, for he said, "I have not the least doubts, it was all for the best. If I had not been ruined, I should never have been a clergyman, never preached a sermon, or written a tract or book."

In spite of all of the trials that Ryle experienced

– financial ruin, loss of three wives, his own poor health – he learned several life lessons. First, care and tend to your own family. Second, swim against the tide when you need to. He was evangelical before it was popular and he held to principles of Scripture: justification by faith alone, substitutionary atonement, the Trinity, and preaching. Third, model Christian attitudes toward your opponents. Fourth, learn and understand church history. Important benefits come from past generations. Fifth, serve in old age; "die in the harness." And, sixth, persevere through your trials.

These were life principles that Ryle learned as he lived his life, as he preached, as he wrote, and as he spread the gospel. He was forever a supporter of evangelism and a critic of ritualism.

J. C. Ryle was recommended by Prime Minister Benjamin Disraeli to be Bishop of Liverpool in 1880 where he then worked to build churches and mission halls to reach the whole city. He retired in 1900 at the age of 83 and died later that year. His successor described him as "a man of granite with a heart of a child."

G. C. B. Davies said "a commanding presence and fearless advocacy of his principles were combined with a kind and understanding attitude in his personal relationships."

Sources:

William P. Farley, "J. C. Ryle: A 19th-century Evangelical," *Enrichment Journal, http://enrichmentjournal.ag.org/200604/200604_120_jcryle.cfm.*

"J. C. Ryle," *The Banner of Truth, https://banneroftruth.org/us/about/banner-authors/j-c-ryle/.*

"J. C. Ryle," *Theopedia, https://www.theopedia.com/john-charles-ryle.*

David Holloway, "J. C. Ryle – The Man, The Minister and The Missionary," *Bible Bulletin Board, http://www.biblebb.com/files/ryle/j_c_ryle.htm.*

Other Similar Titles

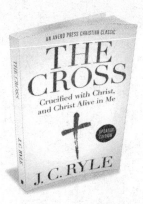

The Cross, by J. C. Ryle

I want to tell you what perhaps the greatest Christian who ever lived (the Apostle Paul) thought of the cross of Christ. Believe me, the cross is one of deepest importance. This is no mere question of controversy; this is not one of those points on which men may agree to differ and feel that differences will not shut them out of heaven. A man must be right on this subject, or he is lost forever. Heaven or hell, happiness or misery, life or death, blessing or cursing in the last day – all hinges on the answer to this question: "What do you think about the cross of Christ?"

Available where books are sold.

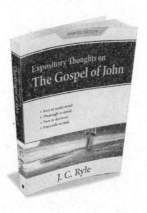

Expository Thoughts on the Gospel of John, by J. C. Ryle

Wisdom, encouragement, and exhortation is contained in these pages. Not because of the author's brilliance, but because of the words of truth contained in the gospel of John. And just as the Apostle John didn't draw any attention to himself, so also J. C. Ryle clearly and wonderfully directs his words and our thoughts towards the inspired words of scripture. If we truly love God, we will love His word; and the more study His word, the more we will love God.

Available where books are sold.

Holiness, by J. C. Ryle

He who wants a correct understanding of holiness must first begin by examining the vast and solemn subject of sin. He must dig down very deep if he wants to build high. Wrong views about holiness are generally traceable to wrong views about human corruption.

Practical holiness and entire self-consecration to God are not given adequate attention by modern Christians. The unsaved sometimes rightly complain that Christians are not as kind and unselfish and good-natured as those who make no profession of faith. Far too many Christians make a verbal proclamation of faith, yet remain unchanged in heart and lifestyle. But Scripture makes it clear that holiness, in its place and proportion, is quite as important as justification. Holiness, without which no one shall see the Lord (Hebrews 12:14). It is imperative that Christians are biblically and truly holy.

Available where books are sold.

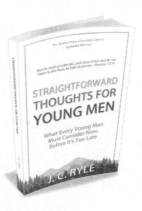

Straightforward Thoughts for Young Men, by J. C. Ryle

Young men, you form a large and very important class in the population of this country; but where, and in what condition, are your souls? I am growing old myself, but there are few things that I can remember so well as the days of my youth. I have a most distinct recollection of the joys and the sorrows, the hopes and the fears, the temptations and the difficulties, the mistaken judgments and the misplaced affections, and the errors and the aspirations which surround and accompany a young man's life. If I can only say something to keep some young man walking in the right way and preserve him from faults and sins, which may hurt his prospects both for time and eternity, I shall be very thankful.

Available where books are sold.